YOUR FUTURE IS IN YOUR HANDS

A PERSONAL GUIDE TO EMPOWERMENT AND CHANGE

GERALD BRADFORD, TERRENCE MORGAN, FRANKLYN SMITH

Your Future Is in Your Hands: A Personal Guide to Empowerment and Change
First Edition Trade Book, 2024
Copyright © 2024 by Gerald Bradford, Terrence Morgan, and Franklyn Smith

All rights reserved. No part of this publication may be reproduced, stored in a retrieval system, or transmitted in any form by any means—electronic, mechanical, photocopy, recording, or otherwise—except for brief quotations in critical reviews or articles, without the prior permission of the publisher, except as provided by U.S. copyright law.

To order additional books:
www.freshstartps.org

ISBN: 978-1-952943-21-8

Editorial and Book Packaging: Inspira Literary Solutions, Gig Harbor, WA

Printed in the USA

*"Every great dream begins with a dreamer.
Always remember, you have within you the strength, the patience,
and the passion to reach for the stars, to change the world."
~Harriet Tubman*

TABLE OF CONTENTS

Introduction		1
Note to Facilitators		3
MODULE 1:	Benefits of Re-entry Planning	9
MODULE 2:	Who Am I?	11
MODULE 3:	Actions/Behaviors/Values	13
MODULE 4:	Actions/Behaviors/Vices	15
MODULE 5:	Communication Styles	17
MODULE 6:	The Effects of Social Media and Music	20
MODULE 7:	Thinking Errors	22
MODULE 8:	Relapse Prevention Planning	33
MODULE 9:	Your Support System	37
MODULE 10:	Relapse Prevention Review	42
MODULE 11:	Your Personal-Centered Plan	46
MODULE 12:	Goals, Positive Activities, and Perspective	57
MODULE 13:	Dealing with Transition	64
MODULE 14:	How Release Works	66
MODULE 15:	Release Planning Preparation Checklist	68
MODULE 16:	Developing Your Release Plan	71
MODULE 17:	Financial Management/Budgeting	74
MODULE 18:	Goals (30 Days)	76
MODULE 19:	Goals (6 Months)	78
MODULE 20:	Goals (1 Year)	80
MODULE 21:	Goals (3 Years)	82
Conclusion		85
About the Authors		87
Acknowledgments		89

INTRODUCTION

No successful business, person, or organization has achieved success without having a plan of action outlining *what* and *how* they were going to achieve their desired goals. Having a plan is simply a part of success—in every area of life.

An individualized transition plan is a written pathway that can serve as a personalized blueprint for achieving your future objectives as you re-enter society after a time of incarceration. This workbook has been created as a tool in your toolkit to assist as you develop your personal transition plan, but also as a way of introducing you to the power of self-knowledge. Our goal is to help you understand how to unlock the true potential of your ability to create the lifestyle you desire for yourself and your family.

This workbook, designed as a Re-Entry Manual for individuals who will be leaving incarceration and returning to their community, can work hand-in-hand with its prequel, *Taking Charge of Your Future*. While similar, *Your Future Is in Your Hands* has some added material and benefits for the participant. If you have already completed the first manual, completing this second manual will allow you to re-visit those themes and concepts with fresh eyes.

The course is comprised of 21 impactful modules that will help you reconnect with yourself—identifying your goals, strengths, and weaknesses, as well as the internal and external barriers that may be preventing you from achieving your goals for a smooth re-entry. We are sure that by the time you complete this workbook, you will become more aware of yourself and have more confidence in your ability to start living a quality, productive, positive life.

The most beautiful aspect of self-knowledge is the personal empowerment you will feel once you begin to realize that the life you desire is within your own grasp. Your future is in your hands! You just need to harness your own strength, understand how to address your weaknesses, and develop your transition plan.

So, let us get started!

NOTE TO FACILITATORS

Thank you for your participation in the vital work of helping individuals who are looking for a "fresh start" in their lives. The Fresh Start PS Organization and the *Your Future Is in Your Hands* course offer participants an opportunity to create a clean slate.

The goal of the facilitator is to empower and motivate participants, to bring out the best of their potential as they navigate re-entry. The 21 modules in *Your Future Is in Your Hands* are designed to be used interactively, either in a one-on-one or a group setting. The course can be self-paced or set up on a schedule (e.g., once a week, bi-weekly, etc.), as desired. We suggest allowing participants time to respond to the prompts and questions in each module on their own, and then discussing their responses during meeting times.

Module 11, in particular, "Developing Your Personal-Centered Plan," requires some extra preparation on the part of the facilitator in helping participants with their person-centered planning.

Person-centered planning (PCP) is an interactive interview between participants. You, the facilitator, should have already prepared your own sample PCP. If not, you may use an existing PCP that is reflective of the participant's life experience.

If you are working with a group, the students should be divided into groups of two; if there is an odd number of participants, the facilitator should work with the student that was left out of the pairing. Try to have students work with someone whom they do not already know. Once students are paired up, have them sign their name on the first page of their PCP plan ("_____'s Places). Have students exchange their books with each other. Now each student should have their partner's PCP.

Each person should write their partner's name at the top of the rest of the pages in this exercise (Places, Choices, etc.). Participants will be interviewing one another for the whole of this exercise and recording one another's answers in the spaces provided.

The facilitator PCP should be working from a completed PCP they can use to illustrate and explain. Try to use a PCP that is appropriate to the age of the group or individual with whom you are working . If you are using this exercise with young people, use a PCP that is written from a young person's point of view. If you are using this exercise for adults, please use a PCP reflective of an older adult's viewpoint.

When facilitating person-centered planning in person, if available, use large, white sheets of paper, or a whiteboard, to draw PCP Places, People Circles, lists of Likes and Dislikes, Strengths/Talents, Choices, Fears/Worries, Dreams, and finally, the Action Plan, for the whole group to see.

Places

The facilitator should share their PCP Places by drawing three concentric circles on the large, white paper or whiteboard (use the example from Module 11 on page 47). Think of the circles as a target with a bullseye: the center is where you spend the most time, the second ring identifies locations you frequent sometimes, and the outer ring is where you go occasionally. For example, participants might include: Center ring—home, second ring—school/work, third ring—friends' houses (specify). Please make sure to encourage participants to really think about where they spend their time.

The facilitator should share the example (or his/her own) wheel with participants, then have the students interview each other and record their partner's responses.

When the students have completed the activity, ask them to turn the page and write their partner's name on the on the top of the next page.

People

Next, share your sample diagram of "PCP People" by drawing three circles (use the example from the workbook on page 48). The middle circle identifies people with whom you spend the most time, the middle circle is people with whom you *frequently* spend time, and the outer circle is people with whom you *sometimes/occasionally* spend time.

For example: center ring—mother/father, brothers, sisters, etc., second ring—friends (be specific), third ring—people with whom you sometimes associate (e.g., coaches, teachers, mentors, extended family). Please make sure to encourage participants to really think about the people with whom they spend their time.

Once you've shared your wheel with participants, have them interview each other and record their partner's responses. When the students have completed the activity, ask them to turn the page and write their partner's name on the top of the next page.

NOTE TO FACILITATORS

Like and Dislikes

Share examples of what a participant might list for likes and dislikes:

Likes: learning, reading, fishing , making friends
Dislikes: two-faced people, dishonest people, politics

For this exercise, you should share your own likes and dislikes (or those on your sample exercise, if it's not your own) as a list. Once the facilitator shares their Likes and Dislikes list with participants, have students interview each other and record their partner's responses.

When the students have completed the activity, ask them to turn the page and write their partner's name on the top of the next page.

Strengths and Talents

Share examples of what a participant might list for strengths/talents: music, speaking , basketball, football, acting, speaking different languages

Similar to the Likes and Dislikes list above, share the list of your own strengths and talents (or those on the sample you are using) with the participant(s). Once the facilitator shares their Strengths and Talents list with participants, have them interview each other and record their partner's responses. When the students have completed the activity, ask them to turn the page and write their partner's name on the top of the next page.

Choices

In this exercise, participants are being asked to share their choices about things like attending school, going to work, working out, eating healthy food, and having positive friends, etc.

You, the facilitator, should share your own list of PCP Choices, or those on the example PCP you are using. Once you've shared your Choices list with participants, have students interview each other and record their partner's responses.

When the students have completed the activity, ask them to turn the page and write their partner's name on the top of the next page.

Fears/Worries

Examples of what a participant might list for fears/worries: death, police, not having enough money to live, "How will I be able to pay the rent?"

You, the facilitator, should share your own Fears and Worries list, or those on the example PCP you are using. Once you've shared your list with participants, have students interview each other and record their partner's responses.

When the students have completed the activity, ask them to turn the page and write their partner's name on the top of the next page.

Dreams

Ask participants to have identify an aspirational dream (or dreams) related to at least one of these subjects: education, family/home life, employment, clean and sober living, etc.

Again, share your own PCP Dreams, or those on your example, as a list. This step is particularly important. Specify that they should list outs dreams for which they can develop an action plan to achieve.

Once you've shared your own Dreams List (or example) with participants, have students interview each other and record their partner's responses.

When the students have completed the activity, ask them to return their partner's PCP Dreams List. Once the original owner has their list, ask them to number the PCP with their most important dream being number 1 on the list.

Action Plan

In some ways, an action plan is a "heroic" act: it helps us turn our dreams into a reality. An action plan is a way to make sure your vision is made concrete. It describes the way you will use its strategies to meet its objectives. An action plan consists of a number of action steps or changes to be brought about in your community.

Each action step or change to be sought should include the following information:

- **What** actions or changes will occur
- **Who** will carry out these changes
- **By when** they will take place, and for how long

NOTE TO FACILITATORS

- **What resources** (i.e., money, staff) are needed to carry out these changes
- **Status** (Active of pending action)

Encourage participants to revisit their Action Plan bi-weekly in order to gauge progress.

Final Words

Your Future Is in Your Hands is intended to be a "take-away" journal that the participant can keep and refer to in the months and years to come as a reminder and accountability tool. Encourage participants to hang onto these books, and to remember that each day is a new day, and a new opportunity for a fresh start.

MODULE 1

Benefits of Re-entry Planning

Having a solid transition or re-entry plan for when the time comes for you to be released, and to return to regular life, is going to be crucial to your success. The period post-incarceration is a critical juncture that can either propel you toward reintegration with your family, community, and the workforce, or increase the likelihood of your returning to old, self-destructive patterns.

A well-crafted plan will address various aspects of your life such as employment, housing, education, and mental health support, providing a structured pathway for you to rebuild your life. There are many benefits for creating and/or using a Personal Release Plan:

- Can help you be successful and stay on track in obtaining your goals for a successful release and transition into the community
- May be helpful in finding and establishing a release address
- Can be used as a personal business plan by you and your support system to keep you focused and on track
- May reduce stress associated with release
- Can improve your stability and reduce the probability of recidivism/returning to a negative lifestyle and prison
- Identifies what community support is out there for you
- Helps you to understand which community support groups can/cannot help you with your transition
- Helps you keep up with the daily schedule you have set for success
- Ensures you have a back-up plan
- Pushes you to be organized and prepared when released
- Highlights the difficulties you may face once you re-enter society

YOUR FUTURE IS IN YOUR HANDS

- ▶ Creates awareness of your community resources (food, clothing, shelter, financial aid, hot meals, etc.)
- ▶ Helps you feel confident about your successful re-entry into society
- ▶ Can serve as a communication tool to use with your counselor, CCO, transition specialist, employer, family, support network, and others

Crafting this plan will require some effort on your part, but it's well worth it! Do what you can. You may be surprised at what you can accomplish on your own, in advance. At the same time, it is highly important to your success that you let friends and associates know what you are trying to do and ask for HELP! If you do not make a Re-entry Plan and use it, then it cannot help you get out and STAY OUT. There is nothing to lose and everything to gain by creating and putting into effect your personal Re-entry Plan.

What are your thoughts about developing a personalized release plan?

_____
_____
_____

What are your top 3 hopes for your transition?

_____
_____
_____

What are your top 3 concerns for your transition?

_____
_____
_____

MODULE 2

Who Am I?

Identity and self-awareness are important—not only identifying the person you *want* to be, but also the person you *were* and who you are *now*. Every person is a work in progress!

Part of being able to move forward in life is the ability to look back at where you've come from. In your own words, how have you seen yourself change? How would you *like* to change? You can have the confidence to know that you have the answers within you.

These questions will help you with some self-identification and self-awareness:

What kind of person were you before your incarceration?

_____

_____

_____

_____

What kind of person are you today?

_____

_____

_____

_____

YOUR FUTURE IS IN YOUR HANDS

What kind of person do you want to be?

_____

_____

_____

_____

How do you want to be remembered?

_____

_____

_____

_____

MODULE 3

Actions, Behaviors, and Values

Definition of "VALUE"

1. A principal or ideal that is intrinsically valuable or desirable
2. An essential standard that inclines one to act or choose to act in one way or another

Our actions and behaviors are dictated by what we value.

What are values?

- Values reflect an individual's concept of right and wrong.
- Principles are the guiding values of our lives. They should lead us to a more ideal world, and our best version of ourselves.
- Values define what is of worth to us, what is beneficial, and what is harmful.
- Values are standards to guide our actions, judgments, and attitudes.

In other words, how we act reflects what we value the most.

In the space provided below, list three (3) values that you have, and three (3) reasons why you value each.

YOUR FUTURE IS IN YOUR HANDS

Value 1:

1. _____

2. _____

3. _____

Value 2:

1. _____

2. _____

3. _____

Value 3:

1. _____

2. _____

3. _____

Based on your own values, what are three (3) positive behaviors that you will engage in on the outside?

1. _____

2. _____

3. _____

MODULE 4

Actions, behaviors, and VICES

Definition of "VICE"

1. An immoral or bad habit or practice
2. Immoral conduct; derived or degrading behavior

Our actions and behaviors are also dictated by our vices.

What are vices?

- Vices are a lapse in adhering to our values.
- They are behaviors that contradict our own morality.
- Vices are weaknesses in willpower given life through action.

In other words, besides being guided by our values and principles, how we act also reflects the vices we are most susceptible to.

Based on your past behaviors, what are three (3) vices that you engaged in prior to your incarceration that you will need to be aware of (and avoid) on the outside?

1. _____

_____

_____

2. _____

_____

_____

3. _____

_____

_____

_____

Can you identify your past reasons for valuing each of these vices? What were the reasons you engaged in them?

Vice 1: _____

Vice 2: _____

Vice 3: _____

MODULE 5

Communication Styles

Most conflicts, whether they are professional or personal, are usually the product of some type of unmet need. If we are unable to articulate (communicate) what the unmet need is, then we can never achieve a positive result that will satisfy the underlying issue. An effective, positive, and professional communicator is one who has developed an understanding of the four basic types of communication styles described below. In this exercise, you will assess which of the four basic styles of communication relates to you. You'll also identify why you believe you are that type of communicator, and which styles of communication you prefer others use when speaking to you.

The Four Basic Styles of Communication

Passive ▶ Aggressive ▶ Passive-Aggressive ▶ Assertive

Passive Communication:

- Individuals develop a pattern of avoiding expressing their opinions or feelings, protecting their rights, and identifying and meeting their needs.
- These individuals do not respond openly to hurtful or anger-inducing situations.
- They instead unknowingly allow grievances and annoyances to build up.
- Once their high tolerance threshold for unacceptable behavior has been reached, they are prone to explosive outbursts, which usually seem out of proportion to the triggering incident.
- They then may return to their passive state after the outburst due to feeling shame, guilt, or confusion.

Common Behaviors of Passive Communicators:

- Failing to assert for themselves
- Allowing others to purposely or unintentionally infringe on their rights
- Failing to express their feelings, needs, or opinions
- Tending to speak softly or apologetically
- Exhibiting poor eye contact and slumped body posture

Aggressive Communication:

- Individuals express their feelings and opinions and advocate for their needs in a way that violates the rights of others. Thus, aggressive communicators are verbally and/or physically abusive.

Common Behaviors of Aggressive Communicators:

- Trying to dominate others
- Using humiliation to control others
- Criticizing, blaming, or attacking others
- Being very impulsive
- Having low frustration tolerance
- Speaking in a loud, demanding, and overbearing voice
- Acting threateningly and rudely
- Not listening well
- Interrupting frequently
- Using "you" statements
- Having an overbearing or intimidating posture

Passive-Aggressive Communication:

- Individuals appear passive on the surface but are really acting out anger in a subtle, indirect, or behind-the-scenes way. These individuals usually feel powerless, stuck, and resentful. They feel incapable of dealing directly with the object of their resentments. Instead, they express their anger by undermining the object (real or imagined) of their resentments.

Common Behaviors of Passive-Aggressive Communicators:

- Muttering to themselves rather than confronting the person or issue
- Having difficulty acknowledging their anger
- Using facial expressions that don't match how they feel (like smiling when angry)
- Using sarcasm
- Denying there is a problem
- Appearing cooperative while purposely doing things to annoy and disrupt
- Using subtle sabotage to get even

Assertive Communication:

- Individuals clearly state their opinions and feelings, and firmly advocate for their rights and needs without violating the rights of others. These individuals value themselves, their time, and their emotional, spiritual, and physical needs and are strong advocates for themselves while being very respectful of the rights of others.

Common Traits of Assertive Communicators:

- They feel connected to others.
- They feel in control of their lives.
- They can mature because they address issues and problems as they arise.
- They create a respectful environment for others to grow and mature.

MODULE 6

The Effects Of Social Media And Music

As human beings, we receive information from three basic sources: family (immediate and extended), community (schools, churches, clubs, etc.), and media (social media, TV, music, videos, etc.). This exercise is to help you identify how social media—as well as music—can influence our attitudes, beliefs, and choices (ABCs) in a positive or negative way. For example, how do these things influence the way we dress? Or the type of people we are attracted to? Or our everyday lifestyle choices?

1. Please describe how much time you spend on social media on any given day.

2. List four impacts/influences that social media has had on you in a positive way.

3. List four impacts/influences that social media has had on you in a negative way.

4. What music/song best describes you? Why?

MODULE 6

5. How does social media and/or certain genres of music make you feel? Please identify your feelings (positive or negative) when you are utilizing these.

6. What are some productive things you can do as a substitute for using social media?

7. How do you think social media, or certain genres of music, can influence a person's attitude, beliefs, and choices?

MODULE 7

Thinking Errors

There are not many people who have been incarcerated that truly want to return to confinement after they are released. Unfortunately, even people who have put serious and intensive efforts into a release plan and have every intention to remain crime free have strayed from the path and regrettably ended up in the same place they were trying so hard to stay away from.

It is important to identify some common poor thinking habits that can lead you back to irresponsible and criminal behaviors. If you can change these poor thinking habits or beliefs to positive and responsible ways of thinking, then your behaviors will change as well.

We change our behaviors by first starting with our thoughts. Did you know that you can control how you behave by the things you say to yourself each day? For example, if you are trying to cut back on how much coffee you drink each day, and you allow your "self-talk" to keep telling you how much you need a cup of coffee and how much better your day would go if you just had another cup of coffee, then most likely you are going to go get another cup of coffee.

The opposite is also true: if you reinforce why you are trying to cut back on drinking things that are unhealthy and encourage your "self-talk" to tell you to have a glass of water so that later in the day you will feel better, then you will be more likely to have some water and eventually the urge to have coffee will evaporate.

The first step to changing your poor thinking habits is to recognize them for what they are. From the time you were born, you have been generating beliefs and observations about the world and people around you and how you fit in. You have developed a unique way of seeing and thinking about everything you have experienced based on the family who raised you and the friends you hung around with.

Change is HARD . . . Changing old habits will be difficult. As you work toward more responsible attitudes and behaviors, a part of your brain will want to react the same way it is used to. This can be an uncomfortable feeling that tries to draw you back to your old ways of doing things. This is a normal feeling when you are attempting to make changes in your life.

Using Mental Movies to Correct Wrong Thinking

"Mental movies" can make this process a little easier. We have all done this! We may not have known there was a formal name for it, but we have all done it. It happens like this: you are in a quiet space and all of a sudden you are thinking back on something that has happened in your life: a recent job interview, a party you were at, an encounter with the police. In your head you are playing back what happened, like a movie in your head. Have you ever wished the ending to the mental movie was a little different than the actual ending? Everyone has at one point or another. You can use these mental movies and turn them into mental *rehearsals*. Mentally rehearsing future situations helps you get more comfortable with a new way of thinking about different situations.

Here's how to be intentional about mental rehearsals:

1. Begin your mental rehearsal by relaxing. Take a few deep breaths and tell yourself to relax.
2. Pick out a situation that has caused you problems in the past. Now create a mental movie in which you act in a rational and responsible way rather than falling back to your old thinking errors.
3. Be ready to take on the uncomfortable feelings you will experience in your mental rehearsal. Concentrate on having positive feelings about your new way of handling the situation.
4. Rehearse your mental movies several times until you start to feel comfortable and confident with your new responses.

Below are several thinking errors that will need to be addressed and corrected in order to effect a successful transition. After we identify each, there will be a "mental rehearsal" exercise to help you make this correction in your thinking. Remember, "rehearsal" also means "practice." You know how the old saying goes: "Practice makes perfect!"

Thinking Error #1 – Making Excuses

One usual form of thinking errors is the tendency to make excuses to justify your own actions or shift blame. Here are some common examples:

- "It's a stupid law. I don't even know why they would even make a law like that."
- "If my public defender knew what he was doing, I wouldn't even be here."
- "If you were in my same situation, you would have done the same thing I did."
- "Hey, if you are stupid enough to leave the keys in your car, then it should be stolen from you. If I didn't do it, then someone else would have."

Does this sound familiar? Describe below two examples of how you have made excuses in the past:

1.

2.

Is this a poor thinking habit that you should work on? ❏ Yes   ❏ No
Explain why or why not:

Ways you can work on changing these thinking errors:

- Admit personal responsibility for the consequences of your actions.
- Understand that life is not always fair and that just because something is unfair, it does not excuse criminal behavior.
- Bravely and honestly look at past failures and future personal goals.
- Try to understand the significance your actions have had on victims, victims' families, family, and the community.

Select one of the examples you wrote above. Play out the same situation in your mind from this situation, but now imagine yourself acting in an honest, responsible, and rational manner. What are you saying to yourself? Make sure you are using self-talk that is positive. Use action-oriented words or phrases. Make your mental video as realistic and personal as possible.

MODULE 7

Mental Rehearsal

Write down your new self-talk for your mental rehearsal. Your new self-talk should not include making excuses, blaming, or justifying. Instead, you are taking personal responsibility.

Thinking Error #2 – Self-Service Acts of Kindness

"Self-serving acts of kindness" is making yourself look good or generous when in reality, you have been neither. Here are some examples:

- "Hey! If you're my friend or family; there is nothing I wouldn't do for you."
- "I would give my mom the shirt off my back if she needed it."
- "Yea, I stole a few cars, but I always made sure it was from someone who could afford it and I'm sure they had insurance."
- "It doesn't matter how I made the money, and besides—I always give a dollar or two to that homeless guy down the street."

Describe 2 examples of how you have justified yourself with self-serving acts of kindness.

1.

2.

Is this a poor thinking habit that you should work on? ❏ Yes   ❏ No
Explain why or why not:

Ways you can work on changing this belief:

- Honestly look back on, and recognize, times that your behavior was destructive.

- Recognize that actions like those in the Disney movie *Robin Hood*—taking from the rich and giving to the poor—does not excuse criminal acts.
- Look back on some of your past actions to honestly find the victims in the crimes you committed and dismissed as victimless.

Select one of the two examples you wrote above. Play out the same situation in your mind from this situation, but now imagine yourself acting in an honest, responsible, and rational manner. What are you saying to yourself? Make sure you are using self-talk that is positive. Use action-oriented words or phrases. Make your mental video as realistic and personal as possible.

Mental Rehearsal

Write down your new self-talk for your mental rehearsal. Your new self-talk should not include using your good deeds to justify your criminal actions, your choices should not be harming others.

Thinking Error #3 – Making Exceptions for Yourself

Most often, this is a sense of being "above the law":

- "After everything they put me through, I deserve this."
- "I can have what I want anytime I want it."
- "If I'm in a hurry, I don't care whom I step on to get in front of the line; they can wait for me."
- "The rules don't apply to me."

Describe 2 examples of how you have felt that you were "above the law."

1.

2.

Is this a poor thinking habit that you should work on?   ❏ Yes   ❏ No
Explain why or why not:

Ways you can work on changing this belief:

- Take inventory of what you have earned, not what you want.
- Take inventory of what is yours and what is not.
- Learn to respect others and their property.
- Try putting yourself in the other person's "shoes."
- Recognize that grown adults do not participate in juvenile behaviors.

Select one of the two examples you wrote above. Play out the same situation in your mind from this situation, but now imagine yourself acting in an honest, responsible, and rational manner. What are you saying to yourself? Make sure you are using self-talk that is positive. Use action-oriented words or phrases. Make your mental video as realistic and personal as possible.

Mental Rehearsal

Write down your new self-talk for your mental rehearsal. Try to identify the difference between your wants and your needs.

Thinking Error #4 – Manipulation and Control

Trying to manipulate or control others to get what we want others is a self-centered behavior often rooted in immaturity and deception. When we use tricks to get what we want, it might work for a short time, but it will ultimately hurt relationships and make people not trust us. It's better to talk openly and find solutions together. Sometimes, it means letting people do their own thing, their own way, even if we're not personally happy about it. That way, everyone feels respected, and we build stronger connections instead of trying to control others.

Describe 2 examples of how you have asserted power over others or manipulated others:

1.

2.

Is this a poor thinking habit that you should work on?   ❏ Yes   ❏ No
Explain why or why not:

Select one of the two examples you wrote above. Play out the same situation in your mind from this situation, but now imagine yourself acting in an honest, responsible, and rational manner. What are you saying to yourself? Make sure you are using self-talk that is positive. Use action-oriented words or phrases. Make your mental video as realistic and personal as possible.

Mental Rehearsal

Write down your new self-talk for your mental rehearsal. View yourself as an equal to others (and they as equals to you), and treat people as you would want to be treated.

Error #5: Lazy Thinking

Lazy thinking is like taking the easy path for your brain. Instead of thinking critically, asking questions, and really *thinking*, it's like using shortcuts and just believing things without checking. It's like when you choose the quickest way instead of the smartest way. But, if you want your brain to be strong and smart, and to make good choices, it's better to ask questions, think hard, and not just go with the first (or easiest) idea that comes to mind.

MODULE 7

Describe 2 examples of when you have had lazy thinking:

1.

2.

Is this a poor thinking habit that you should work on?   ❏ Yes   ❏ No
Explain why or why not:

Select one of the two examples you wrote above. Play out the same situation in your mind from this situation, but now imagine yourself acting in an honest, responsible, and rational manner. What are you saying to yourself? Make sure you are using self-talk that is positive. Use action-oriented words or phrases. Make your mental video as realistic and personal as possible.

Mental Rehearsal

Write down your new self-talk for your mental rehearsal. See yourself following through and celebrating accomplishments both big and small.

Thinking Error #6 – Avoiding Responsibility

Facing up to personal responsibility is an important of maturity, adulthood, and good citizenship in the community. When we admit our mistakes and fix them, we earn trust and respect. When we do the right thing, even if it's hard, we contribute to healthy structure and stability in our families and communities. When we avoid responsibility, we foist it onto someone else, which creates resentment and worse. Dodging responsibility might seem easier, but it just causes more trouble in the long run. Taking ownership shows maturity, demonstrates integrity, and is foundation of good leadership.

Describe 2 examples of how you have ignored your responsibilities.

1.

2.

Is this a poor thinking habit that you should work on?   ❏ Yes   ❏ No
Explain why or why not:

Select one of the two examples you wrote above. Play out the same situation in your mind from this situation, but now imagine yourself acting in an honest, responsible, and rational manner. What are you saying to yourself? Make sure you are using self-talk that is positive. Use action-oriented words or phrases. Make your mental video as realistic and personal as possible.

Mental Rehearsal

Write down your new self-talk for your mental rehearsal. Concentrate on the feeling of getting done the things you have to get done, feel the relief of these things not being on your list of worries anymore. Pay attention to the rewards of your positive actions.

Thinking Error #7 – Feeling Untouchable

Feeling untouchable, or thinking you can avoid consequences, is risky. It may lead to making bad choices, hurting others, and facing trouble. Remember, everyone makes mistakes; thinking you're smarter than others will cause you to trip up sooner or later, and thinking you're invincible will inevitably cause more harm than good. Stay humble, learn from your (and other people's mistakes), heed warnings, and be accountable for your actions.

MODULE 7

Describe 2 examples of how you thought you could get away with anything.

1.

2.

Is this a poor thinking habit that you should work on?   ❏ Yes   ❏ No
Explain why or why not:

Select one of the two examples you wrote above. Play out the same situation in your mind from this situation, but now imagine yourself acting in an honest, responsible, and rational manner.

What are you saying to yourself? Make sure you are using self-talk that is positive. Use action-oriented words or phrases. Make your mental video as realistic and personal as possible.

Mental Rehearsal

Write down your new self-talk for your mental rehearsal. Remember that you are not too slick to get caught in a criminal act. See yourself passing by what used to be an opportunity for crime.

Thinking Error #8 - Distractions

Staying focused on your goals is crucial for success. Avoiding distractions and steering clear of worthless pursuits or bad choices ensures a smoother journey. It's easy to be enticed by immediate pleasures or detours, but these often lead to regrets. By making thoughtful decisions aligned with your aspirations, you will build a foundation for long-term satisfaction and achievement. Keep your priorities in mind, resist tempting shortcuts, and stay committed to the path that leads to your dreams. Remember, every positive choice contributes to a brighter future.

Describe 2 examples of how you have been sidetracked.

1.

2.

Is this a poor thinking habit that you should work on?   ❏ Yes   ❏ No
Explain why or why not:

Select one of the two examples you wrote above. Play out the same situation in your mind from this situation, but now imagine yourself acting in an honest, responsible, and rational manner.

What are you saying to yourself? Make sure you are using self-talk that is positive. Use action-oriented words or phrases. Make your mental video as realistic and personal as possible.

Mental Rehearsal

Write down your new self-talk for your mental rehearsal. Pay attention to what might distract you from your commitments, plans and goals, try to make choices that will allow you to follow through.

MODULE 8

Relapse Prevention Planning

"Failing to plan for your future is planning to fail in the future."

We do not always know what is going to happen. However, when we look at an uncertain future, we can make plans for what we would do in general situations as a way of preparing. It is always helpful to have an idea of how you would react in "what if" situations. Preparation and proper planning lead to success.

Relapse Prevention Support Network

We all choose the people we associate with. We join groups and create families to support others as we ourselves are supported by these networks and/or enter-action. Truly successful people don't become successful on their own. The hardest thing to do for recovering Addicts" (regardless of your addiction) and for most people who are struggling to overcome personal adversities is to pick up the phone and ask for help. Asking for help is extremely difficult. We often think we have all the answers or will be fine on our own. But why does it have to be alone? Ask for help before you need it, and even if you don't think you need it anymore. Ask for it when you think no one can or wants to help you. Why? Because you're wrong; they can, and they will help!

YOUR FUTURE IS IN YOUR HANDS

Ask yourself:

What specific people and types of people do I want around me after release?

_____

_____

_____

What kind of signs do I want my support group to look for in my behavior that

_____

_____

_____

May be warning signs that I'm about to relapse?

_____

_____

_____

What do I want each person from the list above to do for me if I'm in danger of relapsing and coming back to prison?

_____

_____

_____

MODULE 8

What will I do when I feel like relapse is inevitable? When I think there's nothing to do but go back to my old ways?

___

What will I do when I think that no one cares about whether I succeed or not?

___

What will I do when I feel like isolating myself from everyone else and just doing my own thing again?

___

What will I do when I start getting scared that I might relapse and go back to prison?

___

What will I do when I start thinking that I can't make it on the outside and that it would be better to just relapse and go back to my old ways?

_____

_____

_____

MODULE 9

Your Support System

For the most part, we choose the people we associate with. We join groups, make friends, and create families to support one another, as we, too, are supported by these networks and interactions. Truly successful people do not become successful on their own—they utilize and rely on the people around them.

Often the hardest thing to do for anyone endeavoring to overcome personal adversities is to pick up the phone and ask for help. We often think we have all the answers or will be fine on our own. Or, we are embarrassed and ashamed. But we were never meant to do this alone!

Ask for help before you need it, and even if you don't think you need it anymore. Ask for it even when you think no one can or wants to help you. Why? Because you are wrong. They can, they want to, and they will.

In this exercise, please answer the following questions about how your support network can aid you in your transition and recovery:

What specific people and/or types of people do you want to surround yourself with?

1.

2.

3.

YOUR FUTURE IS IN YOUR HANDS

What kind of signs do you want your support group to look for in your behavior that may be warning signs that you are about to relapse?

1.

2.

3.

What do you want each person from the list above to do for you if you are in danger of relapsing or going back to detention/prison?

1.

2.

3.

MODULE 9

> Drugs, alcohol, and negative thinking will destroy you.
> This is a simple yet undeniable fact.
> Support networks, meetings, and groups are there to help you
> beat these types of influences so that you can succeed in life.

Family and Friends: Who do you have in your life that can serve as a healthy supporter?

1.

2.

3.

Mentors: Who are your experienced and trusted advisors?

1.

2.

3.

Support Groups: What interactions do you have for people with similar experiences and who understand what you're going through?

    1.

    2.

    3.

Spiritual and religious (if applicable): How can you stay connected spiritually in your search of hope and purpose in your life?

    1.

    2.

    3.

MODULE 9

Therapy: What professional support do you have lined up to help you work through issues and struggles?

    1.

    2.

    3.

Leisure Activities and interests: What can you be involved in to provides a break with fun, relaxation, and connection to others?

    1.

    2.

    3.

MODULE 10

Relapse Prevention Review

Take some time to review the following important points:

- Criminal behavior has its roots in our beliefs and what we value.
- Beliefs are root to our culture and how we were raised. These types of belief may have had values during that period of time, but now need to be reexamined to see if it still applies.
- Other types of beliefs are based on emotion, not logic, these types of beliefs often are damaging and not useful to our success.
- Negative values lead to negative beliefs which in turn lead to negative behavior.
- Knowing your values helps you know yourself which in turn lets you control your life.
- Be aware of dangerous situations and triggers that may lead to relapse, you can avoid them and stay free.
- Most people spend time identifying the major triggers (people, places, and things) that will influence their behavior, overlooking the minor issues can set the stage for the major issues to happen.
- Become more aware of the minor issues and/or concerns that you have will help you to avoid setting yourself up for the major traps that will lead you back to prison?
- Identify some reservations that you have about your future and/or your future plans that still need to be addressed.
- Having a plan that includes a support group, you can avoid many of the dangers of relapse.

Answer these questions for yourself:

MODULE 10

What past issues brought me to prison and might again?

1.

2.

3.

4.

What situations do I really fear might lead me back to prison?

1.

2.

3.

4.

YOUR FUTURE IS IN YOUR HANDS

Why do these situations seem dangerous to me?

1.

2.

3.

4.

What reservations do I have to overcome?

1.

2.

3.

4.

MODULE 10

How will my support system help me in my reintegration?

1.

2.

3.

4.

MODULE 11

Your Personal-Centered Plan

Person-centered planning (PCP) is a process for selecting and organizing the services and supports that someone may need to live successfully within a community. **Most importantly, it is a process that is directed by the person who receives the support. They make it themselves.**

PCP helps the person construct and articulate a vision for the future, consider various paths, engage in decision-making and problem solving, monitor progress, and make needed adjustments in a timely manner. It highlights individual responsibility, including taking appropriate risks. Emergency planning is also often part of the process.

The PCP approach identifies the individual's places, people, fears, strengths/talents, choices, dreams, and SMART GOAL action plans. Unique factors such as culture and language are also taken into account. These elements are included in a high individualized, unique, written plan for support which will help guide to success.

Person-centered planning should involve every service and support the individual is receiving, such as legal representation, support groups, counseling, and more. These will help define the plan.

INSTRUCTION: This exercise will be done with a partner. Your facilitator will give instructions for competing the following worksheets.

MODULE 11

_____'s places

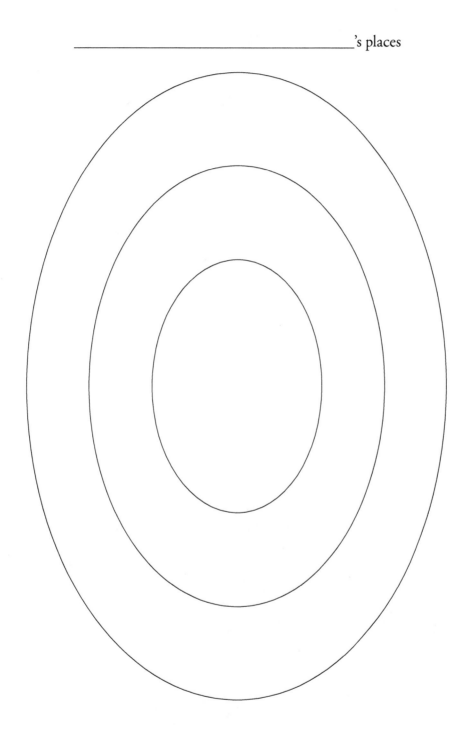

YOUR FUTURE IS IN YOUR HANDS

_____'s people

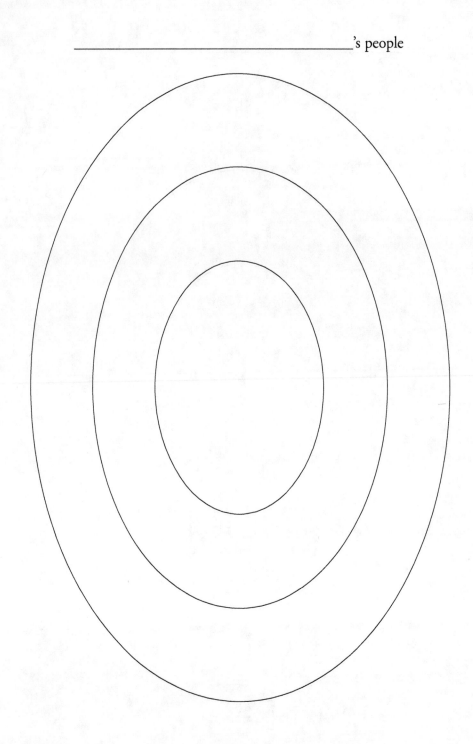

MODULE 11

_____'s fears/worries

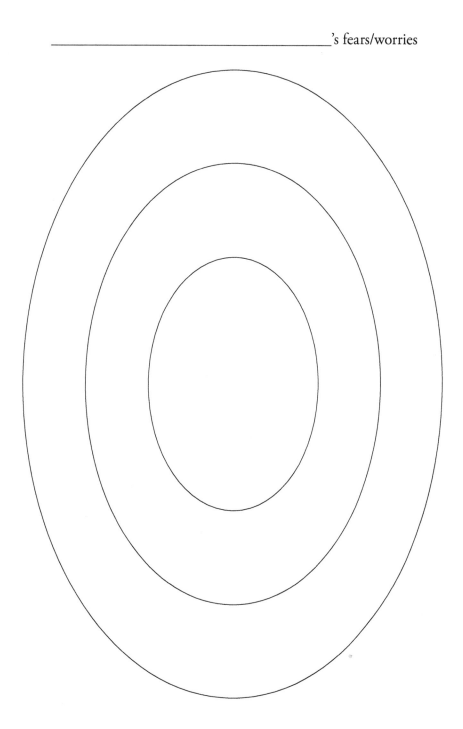

YOUR FUTURE IS IN YOUR HANDS

_____'s strengths/talents

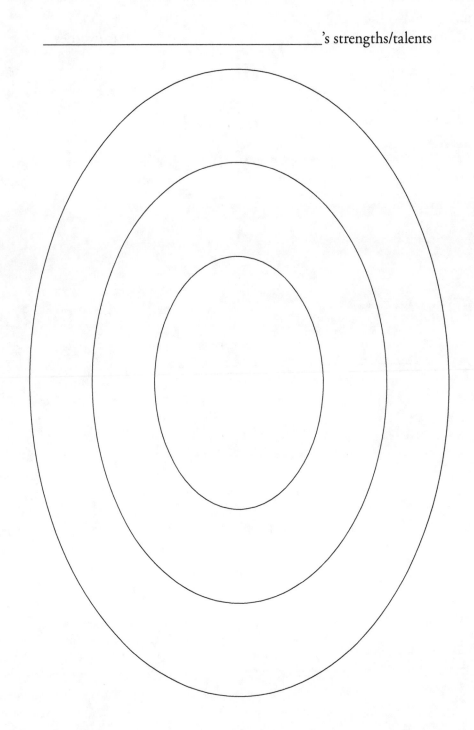

MODULE 11

_____'s choices

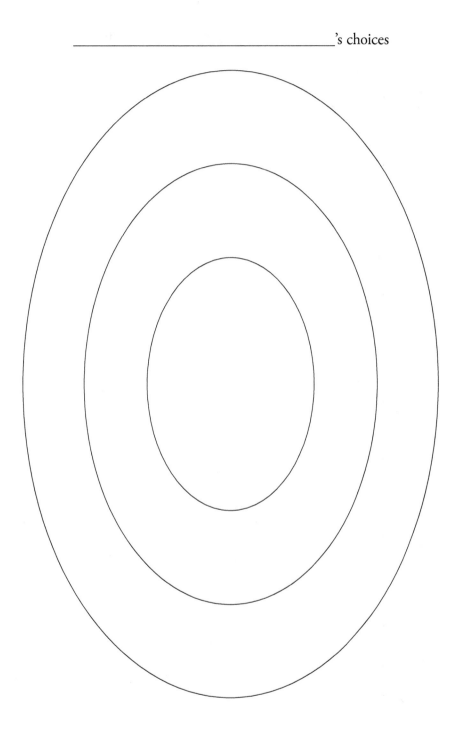

YOUR FUTURE IS IN YOUR HANDS

_____'s dreams

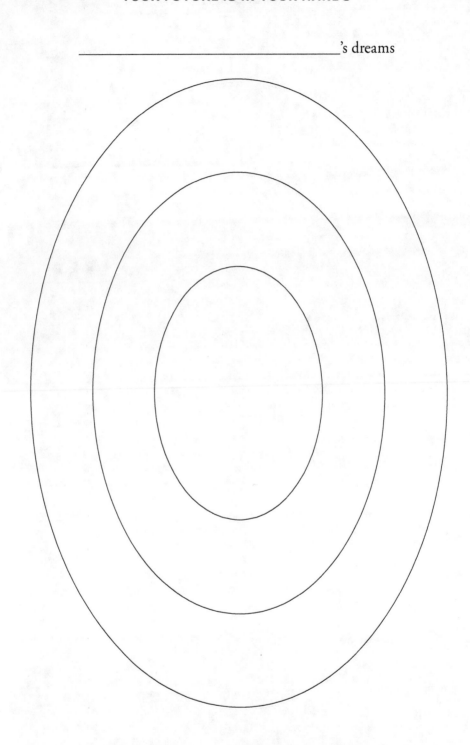

MODULE 11

_____'s action plan

What:	Who:	By When:	Status:

YOUR FUTURE IS IN YOUR HANDS

_____'s action plan

What:	Who:	By When:	Status:

MODULE 11

_____'s action plan

What:	Who:	By When:	Status:

YOUR FUTURE IS IN YOUR HANDS

_____'s action plan

What:	Who:	By When:	Status:

MODULE 12

Goals, Positive Activities, and Perspective

Having a release plan is an important part of being ready to be released from prison. Don't just plan for survival—have long-term goals in mind like education and savings. Plan to be self-sufficient. You are the author and creator of your plan!

Take some time to think through the following questions and answer them for yourself:

What practical thing do I want to do when I get back home, or am settled in my new home?

1.

2.

3.

4.

YOUR FUTURE IS IN YOUR HANDS

What do I need to do to have a successful life?

1.

2.

3.

4.

What kinds of things do I want to do for fun?

1.

2.

3.

4.

MODULE 12

What is going to scare off boredom and make my life worth living?

    1.

    2.

    3.

    4.

What are my goals for my release?

    1.

    2.

    3.

    4.

5.

What actions do I want to define me? What do I want people to see me doing?

1.

2.

3.

4.

5.

What actions do I *not* want to define me? What do I not want people to see me doing?

1.

2.

MODULE 12

3.

4.

5.

What will a person do if they define their release as too hard or difficult to succeed at?

1.

2.

3.

4.

5.

YOUR FUTURE IS IN YOUR HANDS

What will a person do if they define their release as a stepping stone to greater things?

1.

2.

3.

4.

5.

How is my life going to change from what it was?

1. What was my life like before prison?

2. What do I want to change?

3. What am I going to do to make these changes happen?

MODULE 12

4. What will I do to slow down and relax when stress comes?

5. What do I need to address about myself before I get back home? What old thinking or behaviors could hurt me or the ones I care about?

6. What kind of mindset would I need to have in order to be 100 percent sure I would never return to prison?

MODULE 13

Dealing with Transition

Any transition between different environments causes stress—it's a natural reaction. However, this stress can be a trigger that sends us into a relapse. We must learn coping mechanisms to recognize it and handle it in a positive way. This stress does not need to halt all the progress we've made. We can learn to recognize triggers, address them, and continue on our plan.

Honestly answer the following questions:

1. What concerns do I have about adjusting once I get home?

2. What troubles have I experienced in adapting to new places, people or situations in the past?

3. What have I done before to get through stressful times?

4. Can I use the same behaviors as I have in the past when dealing with stressful times?

MODULE 13

5. How will I deal with the feelings of stress such as feeling numb, lost, or overwhelmed?

6. How will I deal with the fear of not being able to make it, find a job, stay off drugs, or any other negative thoughts and self-talk?

7. How will I deal with the depression that comes from expectations not being met and from the natural pressure of change?

8. How will I deal with anger and frustration when my expectations are not met, or when I experience resentment about losing part of my life to prison?

9. How will I deal with the stress of trying to do too much too soon?

10. What negative things about prison do I want to remember, the things that really bothered me there, as a way of avoiding going back? (You may start to think about how much easier it was in prison than being on the outside. At times like these, it helps to remind yourself of why you want to stay out of prison.)

MODULE 14

How Release Works

Your Classification Counselor and Librarian are your primary links to the outside and the DOC system while you are still in prison. It is part of your counselor's responsibility to assist you in preparing for your release.

Tips for collaborating with your counselor:

1. Do not disrespect anyone if obtaining information takes longer than you think it should take. Just be patient and keep trying; this is just one of a lot of tasks that will not necessarily happen when you believe they should happen.
2. Start as early as possible—do not wait until your last few months.
3. Make a list of what you will need to succeed and then divide it into two categories.

What can I accomplish on my own?

What will I need my Classification Counselor and Librarian's assistance with?

1. Be specific and do your research ahead of time. Find names, addresses, and phone numbers and possibly contact people. This will help decrease the time needed when entering the contact phase.
2. Do not expect your counselor to do or know everything—network with other people to help you.
3. Show initiative—develop a Release Plan. This will show that you know what you want to do once released and are starting to execute the process prior to entering the community.

MODULE 14

Questions to ask yourself:

1. What do I need from my counselor?

2. When do I need it?

3. What have I already done to start the process and make it easier for my counselor to help me?

Use the following space to record any contact info or notes you may want to take while looking resources up in the library. Ask the librarian for help.

Believe in yourself and all that you are. Know that there is something inside you that is GREATER than any obstacle!

MODULE 15

Release Planning Preparation Checklist

Identification

Do you have a Social Security card? ❏ Yes ❏ No   Birth Certificate? ❏ Yes ❏ No

Other ID? ❏ Yes ❏ No What? _____

Residence

Do you know where you will be living?   ❏ Yes   ❏ No

Do you need assistance in obtaining housing?   ❏ Yes   ❏ No

Contact Information

Home Number: _____   Cell Number: _____

Message Phone Number: _____   Email Address: _____

Transportation

Do you bus pass?   ❏ Yes   ❏ No

Do you have a vehicle?   ❏ Yes   ❏ No

MODULE 15

Employment

Do you know where you will be working or have any job leads, ideas, and/or offers?   ❏ Yes   ❏ No

Who will you work for? (Name / phone number) _____

Where? (Address, City, State, etc.) _____

What type of work will you do? _____

Education

Do you have a GED?   ❏ Yes   ❏ No

Do you want to do vocational training"   ❏ Yes   ❏ No

What are your career goals? _____

Programs

Have you completed any treatment programs?   ❏ Yes   ❏ No

Were you given a referral for aftercare?   ❏ Yes   ❏ No   MEDICAL

Do you have Affordable Health Care or ACA?   ❏ Yes   ❏ No

Legal

Do you Owe LFO's?   ❏ Yes   ❏ No

Will you be on supervision?   ❏ Yes   ❏ No

YOUR FUTURE IS IN YOUR HANDS

Financial

What debt do you have when you are released? Child support _____ Loans _____

Back mortgage payments or utility bills _____ Loans _____ Restitution _____

Court costs/fines _____ Civil Judgments _____ Tickets _____

Children

Do you have any children?   ❏ Yes   ❏ No   How many? _____   Ages? _____

When was the last time you had contact with your children? _____

Other Services

Are you a veteran?   ❏ Yes   ❏ No

What type of discharge did you receive? _____

Are you a Native American?   ❏ Yes   ❏ No

What tribe/nation do you belong to? _____

Are you actively involved in an organization or religious group?   ❏ Yes   ❏ No

MODULE 16

Developing Your Release Plan

The following builds on what we've covered up to this point in this course, and can be used as a guideline for developing your Personal Transition Plan.

Introduction: Your introduction is a summary of who you are and what kind of life you see yourself living in the future. In reviewing this summary, the reader should be able to see:

1. Know where you would like to be in one year, two years, or three years.
2. Know what your short/long-term goals are.
3. Know how you are planning to achieve your stated goals.
4. Know what resources you will need to assist you in successfully achieving your over-all plan. The answers to the "Who am I?" worksheet can help you with your introduction.

Support System (Network): This is a group of people, i.e., friends, extended family, colleagues and/or professionals that you can count on for help when you when need it. These are the individuals that you feel comfortable going to for accurate up to date information and/or advice when you need to make informed decisions? The answers to the "Support System" worksheet can help you with your Support System Network.

Family Support: Who in your family can you really count on? Here you only want to list the biological and extended family members that you can count on to be there for you. These are the family members who will encourage and help you make informed decisions that is in the best interest of yourself and the family? The answers to the "Support System" question above can help you identify your Family Support.

Release Address: What are your housing options; Homeless Shelter, Community Base Transitional Housing Program (Salvation Army, Etc.), Transitional Housing (Family, Friends, and Clean/Sober), and Permanent (Apt/Home)? List at least 3 housing options that will be available to you.

1.

2.

3.

Education: List any/all certificates, GED, diploma, and/or degrees that you have obtained? These documents will be added to accompany your personalized release plan.

Employment History/Opportunities: List any /all previous employment history, opportunities, and/or employment leads that you will pursue? These documents will be added to accompany your personalized release plan.

MODULE 16

Finances/Support: Make a list of all your first line of financial support once released: family, friends, DSHS, SSI assistance. The answers to the "Support System" worksheet can help you with your Family Support.

Hobbies/Interests: List of the hobbies and relaxing activities that you will be involved in once released.

Motivation: List some of the self-help or motivational activities and/or people that you will be engaged and/or involve with following your release.

Real talk to encourage change: List some of the pro-social activities and people with whom you will be involved with who not be afraid to have real conversations with you in order to continue the process of fostering change and growth following your release.

MODULE 17

Financial Management / Budgeting

How good are you at managing your money? Creating a budget and staying within your budget will be one of the most important aspects of your transition. To manage your money, you need to know exactly how much money you have (and make sure you never spend more than you have coming in!).

In the two columns below, we will look at your income and expenses both presently and in the future. Your instructor can help you fill in the blanks if you are unsure of the actual amounts.

MODULE 17

Income

Wages, Salaries, Tips	$_____
Alimony	$_____
Child Support	$_____
TANF	$_____
WIC	$_____
Food Stamps	$_____
SSI	$_____
SSDI	$_____
Unemployment	$_____
Pension/Annuities	$_____
VA Benefits	$_____
General Relief Assist.	$_____
Dividend Income	$_____
Business (Partner)	$_____
Capital Gain	$_____
Other Misc. Income	$_____
Total Monthly Income	$_____

Expenses

Housing	$_____
Utilities	$_____
Food	$_____
Personal Care	$_____
Clothing	$_____
Phone	$_____
Transportation (car)	$_____
Gas	$_____
Insurance	$_____
Payment	$_____
Transportation (bus)	$_____
Laundry	$_____
Child Support	$_____
Child Care	$_____
LFO's/Debt	$_____
Misc. (credit card)	$_____
Misc.	$_____
Total Expenses	$_____

Calculate Disposable Income

Monthly Income $_____   Monthly Expenses $_____ = Disposable Income $_____

MODULE 18

Your 30-Day Goals

In-order for you to maximize your plan, you need to be strategic with your time and the people you are spending time with.

In this exercise, please list all the activities, events, achievements, and milestones that you would like to accomplish within the first 30 days of your transition. Try to keep it simple!

My goals for the first 30 days of my transition:

1. _____
2. _____
3. _____
4. _____
5. _____
6. _____
7. _____
8. _____
9. _____
10. _____
11. _____

MODULE 18

12. _____
13. _____
14. _____
15. _____
16. _____
17. _____
18. _____
19. _____
20. _____

MODULE 19

Your Six-Month Goals

By the time you reach the six-month mark, you need to start defining your plan and become more strategic with identifying all the "what/why/where/when/how" of your plan.

In this exercise, identify below your "What?" (your desire goal), your "Why?" (did you choose this goal), your "Where?" (do go to accomplish this goal), your "When?" (are you going to start), and your "How?" (will you complete this goal).

Six months after transition I see myself as:

What: _____

_____

_____

Why: _____

_____

_____

MODULE 19

Where: _____

_____

_____

When: _____

_____

_____

How: _____

_____

_____

Resources needed: _____

_____

_____

MODULE 20

Your One-Year Goals

In this exercise, answer the question to identify where you would like to be by the end of the first year of your plan. What changes would you like to see in yourself in your attitude and behavior? What about your employment or family situations?

One year after transition I see myself:

Where: _____

_____

_____

What: _____

_____

_____

Why: _____

_____

_____

MODULE 20

When: _____

_____

_____

How: _____

_____

_____

Resources needed: _____

_____

_____

MODULE 21

Your Three-Year Goals

In this exercise, answer the questions to identify where you would like to be by the end of the third year of your plan. How would you like to see yourself and your lifestyle change beyond the immediate future? How do you see your family? Your career?

Three years after transition, I see myself:

Where: _____

_____

_____

What: _____

_____

_____

Why: _____

_____

_____

MODULE 21

When: _____

_____

_____

How: _____

_____

_____

Resources needed: _____

_____

_____

CONCLUSION

Well done on completing this course. You are now much better equipped to truly "take charge of your future!"

As a reminder, it's important to acknowledge that part of being able to move forward is the ability to look back at where you have come from. This workbook was created to be a self-help journey to understanding yourself on a deep and authentic level. In Module 2, we asked you to identify in your own words how you see yourself.

In this exercise, we are asking the same questions we asked in Module 2, as a way of introducing you to the power of the change, growth, and confidence that has increased since you started this journey. Now, you are connected to the power of self-awareness through developing your Personalized Smart Goals Plan. Let's see how your thinking and outlook have changed since undertaking this course.

Re-asking the Question: *Who Am I?*

What kind of person were you before your current situation?

What kind of person are you today?

What kind of person do you want to be?

YOUR FUTURE IS IN YOUR HANDS

How do you want to be remembered?

What kind of impact would you like to make on the world? On your family and community?

What words of advice would you give to your younger self, based on what you've learned?

ABOUT THE AUTHORS

Gerald Bradford was born and raised in Seattle, Washington, and attended Garfield High School and the University of Washington.

Upon college graduation, Gerald intended on going to law school, but instead fell in love with working with people. He discovered he was passionate about helping individuals move forward with their lives.

After serving with the King County Juvenile Detention Center as an employment counselor, Gerald began working as a counselor with gang members in South Seattle and the Central District. Since then, he's been serving the community in a variety of different ways as a mentor, coach, counselor, uncle, brother, and friend.

In 2005, Gerald began working in re-entry service for the King County Jail—counseling men and women on continuing their education, finding a career, and settling into a positive and productive lifestyle after incarceration. For 15 years, he has been working with adult populations and was the first ever Education and Employment Navigator hired by the State of Washington.

Gerald currently works as the Re-Entry Manager at Renton Technical College and is a founding member of Fresh Start Professional Services and Seattle Peace and Safety Initiative. He is currently serving as the Vice President of the Central District Preservation Authority (CDCPDA).

Terrence L. Morgan is the CEO and Co-Founder of Fresh Start Professional Services. Born and raised in Seattle, Terrence attended and graduated from Seattle Public Schools and received his Associate degree from Pierce College.

Terrence has dedicated his life to educating and assisting individuals impacted by the criminal justice system and is passionate about preparing them for their return into the community and navigating the multiple systems at play. For the last decade, Terrence has worked in the community service field, focusing on the needs of people coming out of prisons, jails, homelessness, family reunification, and domestic violence. Terrence has partnered with the YMCA, Juvenile Justice, Department of Corrections (DOC), and Greenhill High School.

Terrence has a vision to help bring equality to people of color and the BIPOC communities through empowerment, building community, education, career-based employment, and supporting community businesses. His experience as co-author of *Taking Charge of Your Future*, which was offered to the Washington State DOC population under a different title for a period of five years—along with his skills in system navigation and community resources allocation—earned him a leadership position with the Urban League of Metropolitan Seattle, which in turn led to a position as the Workforce Development Program Manager overseeing their Career Bridge Program. He is currently working as a Lead Case Manager for Adonai Employment and Counseling, serving King, Snohomish, and Pierce Counties in Washington State.

Franklyn R. Smith is well-known for his work of more than 15 years in developing productive pathways for adults in transition to obtain the essential supports necessary to experience a successful transition from homelessness, incarceration, and treatment programs (e.g., housing, food, clothing, employment, and pro-social). He was born and raised in Seattle, WA, graduated from Seattle Public Schools, and holds a degree in Business/Accounting with certificates in Supervisory Management, Leadership, Advance Correction Case Management, Workforce Development, WA/DBHA Peer Support Counseling, and Credible Messenger Trainings.

Franklyn is currently the Director of Community Resources at Freedom Project WA and Co-Founder of Fresh Start Professional Service (NPPSC) in Seattle, WA. In 2014, Franklyn developed a Supportive Transitional Re-Entry Model that was presented to the BJA/WA-DOC Second Chance Re-Entry Pilot Project Steering Committee. In 2015, he was the first formerly justice-involved individual to be hired by the WA/DOC as a Community Resources Program Manager and Correction Specialist 3/Re-Entry Navigator. He is also the co-creator of Sober Solutions Transitional Housing LLC, and has consulted in developing Divinity, RAZ Community Services and several other transitional housing programs.

ACKNOWLEDGMENTS

This book is a product of our labor of love toward assisting men and women who want to effect a positive change in their lives, but are struggling to achieve mental and physical liberation, growth, and personal empowerment.

The authors would like to thank all the brothers and sisters whom we have been blessed to assist on their individual journeys toward achieving direction, growth, happiness, personal empowerment, and liberation. It has been an honor and pleasure to be of service to each of you!

We would also like to express our heartfelt appreciation to Ms. Xandis Phillips, the Washington State Dept. of Correction 2nd Chance Reentry Project Team—Mr. James Harms, Mrs. Misty Liles-Patterson, and Ms. Susan Piccinini—for believing in the power of lived experience and working alongside the authors as we presented this curriculum to the men living with-n the confines of the Washington State Department of Corrections.

Lastly, we would like to relay a special thank you to our friend Ms. Jennifer Pace for her contribution to this work, "Thinking Errors," and to highlight her years of service to the citizens of Washington State.

Jennifer, thank you for all that you do!

Jennifer Pace, a dedicated professional for 24 years, has been instrumental in aiding the transition of Washington State returning citizens. Formerly with the Washington State Employment Security Department, she served as Supervisor/Facilitator at Pine Lodge Pre-Release, targeting long-term incarcerated individuals in the Restorative Justice Inmate Program. At Airway Heights Corrections Center, she spent nine years facilitating workshops, coordinating job/resource fairs, and leading informational seminars.

In 2012, Jennifer transitioned to a community-focused role, partnering with Spokane WorkSource, Spokane Action Neighborhood Partners

(SNAP), and the Department of Corrections on the Department of Labor and Industries REXO grant. She assisted recently released citizens in their transition. In 2013, she initiated the Spokane Community Partners for Transition Solutions coalition, uniting community partners for reentry services.

Currently a Re-entry Navigator with Washington State's Department of Corrections Reentry Division, Jennifer guides individuals in planning and implementing their Individual Re-entry Plans, offering valuable community resources. In a temporary project, she facilitates Re-entry Simulations for Department of Corrections Staff, Community Partners, and the incarcerated population, significantly contributing to their re-entry plans. Jennifer Pace remains a steadfast advocate for successful community reintegration.

Printed in the USA
CPSIA information can be obtained
at www.ICGtesting.com
CBHW080758290424
7703CB00002B/4

9 781952 943218